Book

MW00559613

IN RECITAL™
Duets
Volume One

ABOUT THE SERIES • A NOTE TO THE TEACHER

The *In Recital*™ *Duets* series focuses on fabulous duet repertoire intended to motivate your students. All volumes of *In Recital*™ address the issue of motivating students with attainable goals. The comprehensively leveled curriculum makes that possible, and this duet series offers a wonderful repertoire opportunity for your students. You will find original duets, duet arrangements of popular pieces, and duet arrangements of famous classical themes. There are equal-part duets as well as unequal-part duets that can be played by the teacher or a more advanced student. The duets in this series address a wide variety of different musical and technical issues, giving you the selection needed to accommodate your students' needs and plan recital repertoire for the entire year. The series provides practice tips, rehearsal suggestions, and duet performance strategies to help your students be successful!

Use the enclosed CD as a teaching and motivational tool. Have your students listen to the recording and discuss interpretation with you! To learn how to use the CD as a valuable practice aid, turn to page 48.

Production: Frank J. Hackinson
Production Coordinator: Philip Groeber
Art Direction: Terpstra Design, San Francisco, in collaboration with Helen Marlais
Cover and Inside Illustrations: Keith Criss
Engraving: Tempo Music Press, Inc.
Printer: Tempo Music Press, Inc.

ISBN 1-56939-518-7

ORGANIZATION OF THE SERIES
IN RECITAL™ DUETS

The series is carefully leveled into the following six categories: Early Elementary, Elementary, Late Elementary, Early Intermediate, Intermediate, and Late Intermediate. Each of the works has been selected for its artistic as well as its pedagogical merit.

Book Four — Early Intermediate, reinforces the following concepts:

- Students play pieces with dotted-quarter notes followed by eighth notes and sixteenth notes.

- Reinforcement of blocked and broken chords and intervals in left-hand accompaniment patterns.

- An introduction to the blues style.

- Students play pieces in hand positions that expand larger than a fifth.

- Music terms employed are the following: *sforzando*, *a tempo*, *pp*, *ff*, *D.C. al coda*.

- One-octave arpeggios in one hand.

- Rolled chords.

- A variety of major and minor keys.

THE BENEFITS OF PLAYING DUETS

Duets are good for a student's sense of rhythm and ensemble. They learn to "catch" the rhythm — whether it is fast or slow, and they learn to listen to each other and produce subtle changes in dynamics and tempo. Furthermore, playing duets gives students the opportunity to sense their partner's musicianship. The hands-on experience of interacting with another musician and enjoying each other's spirit in the music is an important step in developing their understanding of musicality. Duets can be an integral ingredient in lighting the musical fire!

An ensemble recital is great fun, and a mixed program of solos and duets provides variety for the audience. Playing duets for friends, family, other students, or for school is a wonderful way to spread the joy of music.

Enjoy all of these wonderful duets!

Most of the pieces in this book were arranged as equal-part duets. The only two that are unequal-part duets, with the *secondo* part to be played by the teacher or a more advanced student, are *Hava Nagila* and *St. Louis Blues*.

FF1613

TABLE OF CONTENTS

Primo parts played by Christine Kim; Secondo parts played by Helen Marlais.

A Special Note to Students:

For centuries, people have played duets together. Without movies, television, or stereo, pianists of all ages would come together and play as a great source of entertainment. The most popular orchestral pieces, operas, and advanced piano works were often written for four-hands at one piano, called the "piano duet." This way everyone could enjoy the music of the day right at home!

This collection of duets is for you to play and enjoy! All of the duets are different in character, and each creates a different mood for you as well as for the audience!

Tips for Practicing at Home:

Here are a few practice suggestions for you to do at home. They will help you play these duets successfully with a partner:

1) Practice your part until you can play it without stopping (with correct notes and steady rhythm) before you go to your lesson.

2) Mark in specific starting locations throughout each duet to make your rehearsal easier and more effective. Start at these various locations when you practice at home so you will be ready for your rehearsal.

3) Listen to the CD recording so that you can hear the complete duet. In order to prepare well, listen to the tempo, rhythm, dynamics, articulations, and overall ensemble playing.

Tips for Practicing with your Duet Partner:

1) In order for the ensemble to work well and look professional, start with your hands in your lap. You and your partner should bring your hands up to the keyboard at the same time. Breathe together to begin the duet for perfect synchronization! (Don't count off.)

   After playing, both you and your partner should end with your hands in your lap. Then you are ready to stand and bow after the performance, which you should also practice together.

2) Decide with your ensemble partner who has the melody at any given moment. Ask yourselves, "Which part should be brought out over the other part?"

   After you have played the duet, ask yourselves, "What was the balance like between the melody and the accompaniment throughout the entire piece?"

3) While you are practicing, you might wish to count together; this way you'll be sure to play together at the same tempo and without stopping.

4) Poise at the piano — decide with your partner how you will walk on stage, stand at the piano, and bow to the audience. If you practice this often, you will be very polished at the performance!

5) Discuss with your partner which person can turn each page more easily and practice this well. This is one mark of true professionalism as a duet team. The more nodding and breathing you can do together, the more in sync your pieces will be. Nodding and breathing are good ways to synchronize your timing, just don't overdo it. It should not take attention away from the music. Instead, practice enough so that you can naturally feel each other's pulse and musical gestures.

6) If you have the opportunity to have a page-turner, practice nodding to indicate your page turns. You should not say anything or make any sound that takes the listener away from the music.

7) Really listen to your duet partner's part so you both play completely together.

   Above all, enjoy making music with another person! If you are having trouble with specific parts of the duets, practice more at home so you can concentrate on the musical aspects in rehearsal.

MOURNING DOVES

Secondo

Valerie Roth Roubos

FF1613

MOURNING DOVES

Primo

Valerie Roth Roubos

Secondo

Primo

TWO GUITARS

Secondo

Traditional
arr. Edwin McLean

Lively tango style (♩ = 144-160)

FF1613

TWO GUITARS

Primo

Traditional
arr. Edwin McLean

Secondo

Primo

Hava Nagila

Secondo

Hebrew Folk Song
arr. Melody Bober

With energy (♩ = 168)
2nd time faster

FF1613

HAVA NAGILA

Primo

Hebrew Folk Song
arr. Melody Bober

Secondo

Primo

Secondo

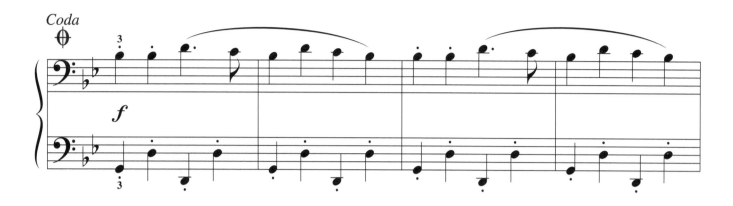

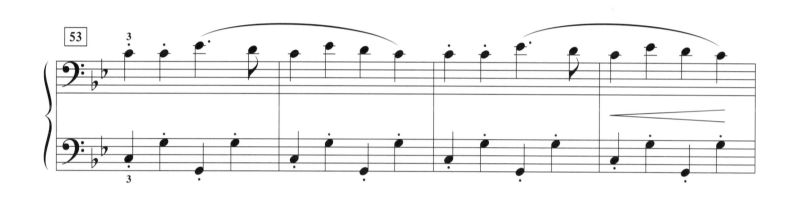

FF1613

Primo

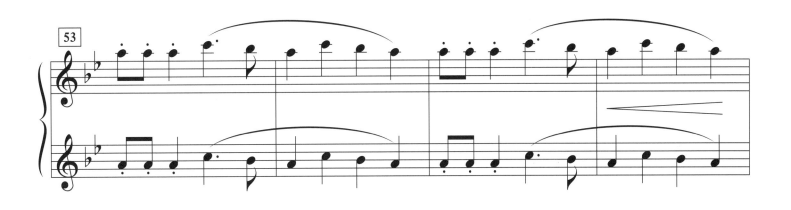

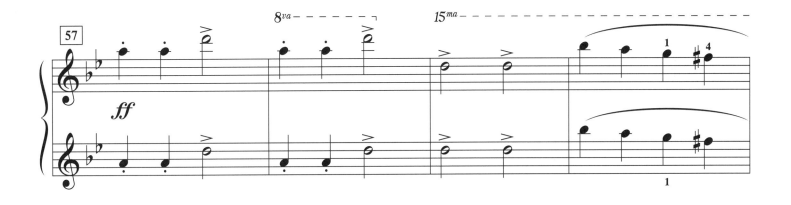

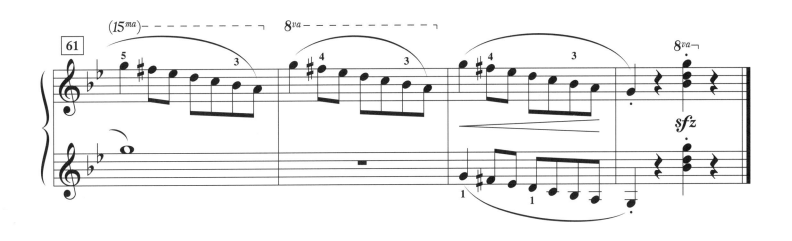

Fascination

Secondo

F. D. Marchetti
arr. Kevin Olson

Graceful waltz tempo (♩ = 126)

FF1613

Fascination

Primo

F. D. Marchetti
arr. Kevin Olson

FF1613

Secondo

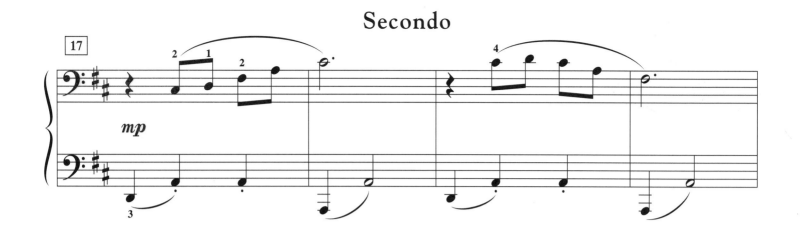

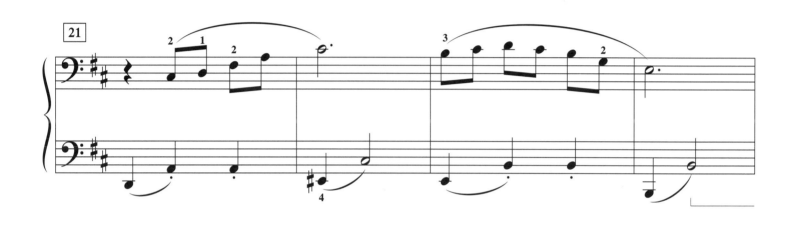

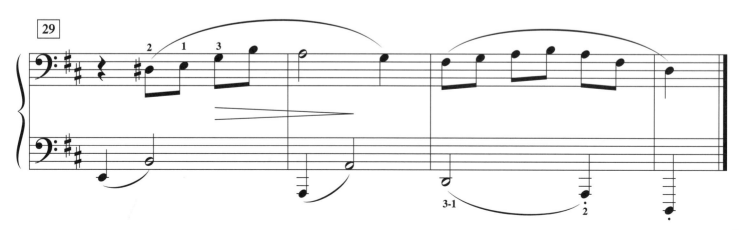

Primo

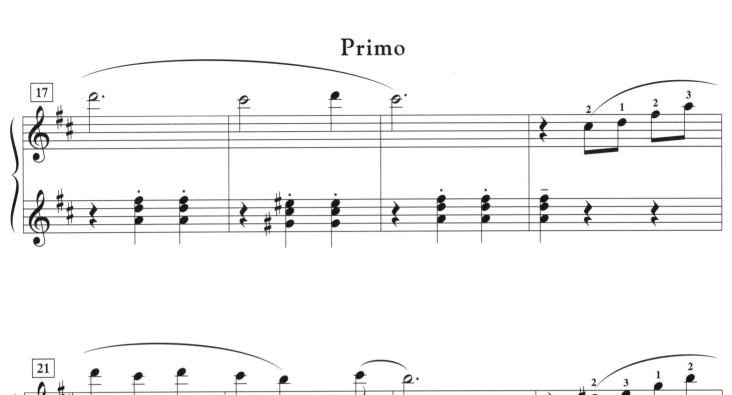

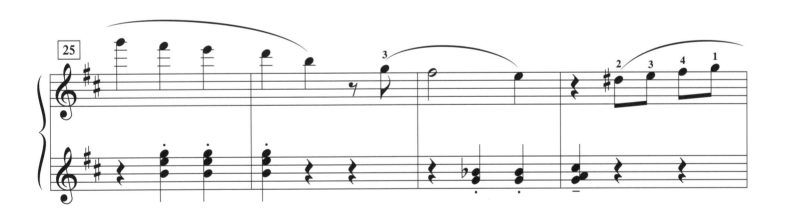

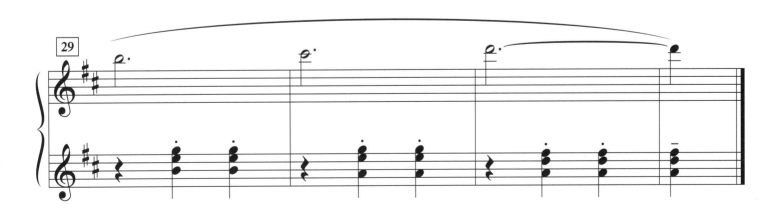

EINE KLEINE NACHTMUSIK

(A Little Nightmusic, K.525)

Secondo

Wolfgang Amadeus Mozart
arr. Timothy Brown

FF1613

EINE KLEINE NACHTMUSIK

(*A Little Nightmusic, K.525*)

Primo

Wolfgang Amadeus Mozart
arr. Timothy Brown

FF1613   International Copyright Secured.   Made in U.S.A.   All Rights Reserved.

Secondo

Primo

ST. LOUIS BLUES

Secondo

William Christopher Handy
arr. Kevin Olson

FF1613

ST. LOUIS BLUES

Primo

William Christopher Handy
arr. Kevin Olson

Secondo

Primo

Northern Expedition

Secondo

Wynn-Anne Rossi

With energy (♩ = ca. 176)

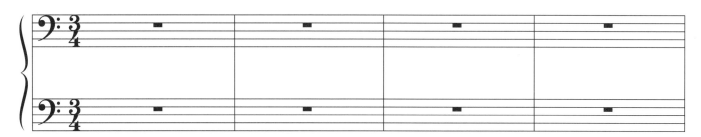

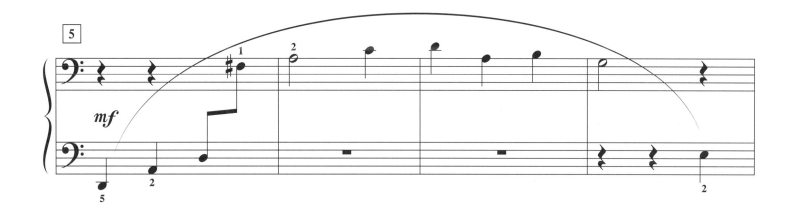

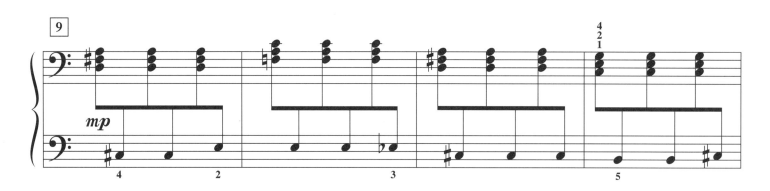

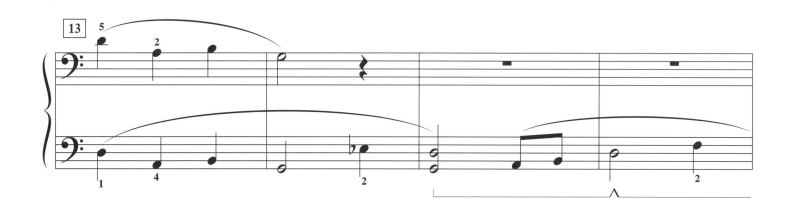

FF1613

NORTHERN EXPEDITION

Primo

Wynn-Anne Rossi

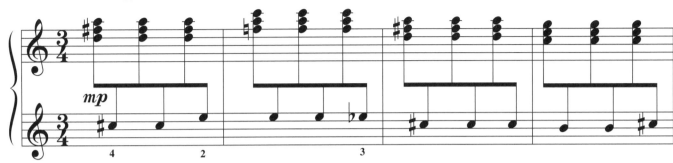

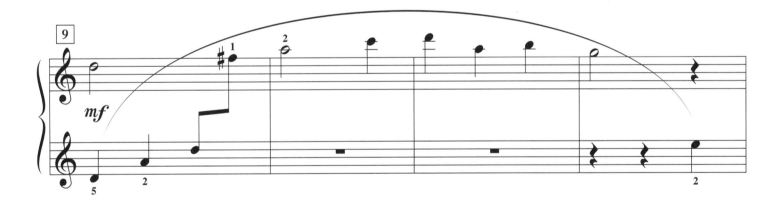

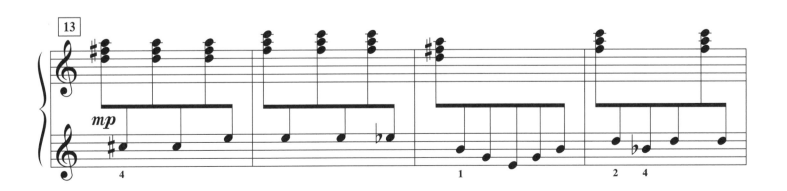

Secondo

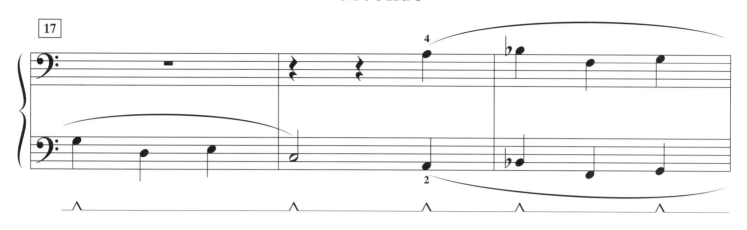

ped. simile

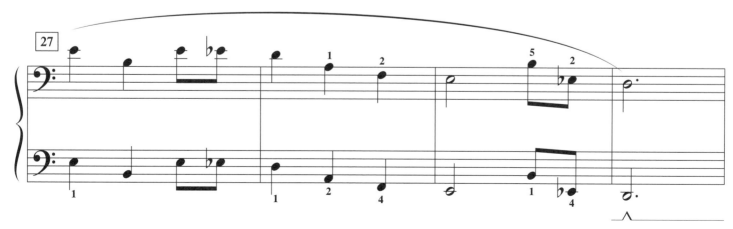

FF1613

Primo

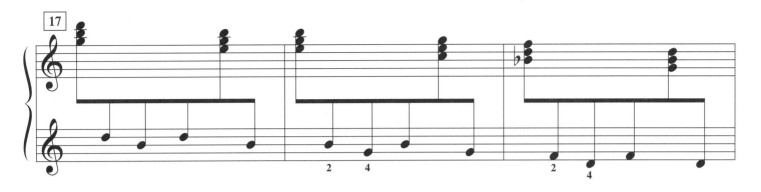

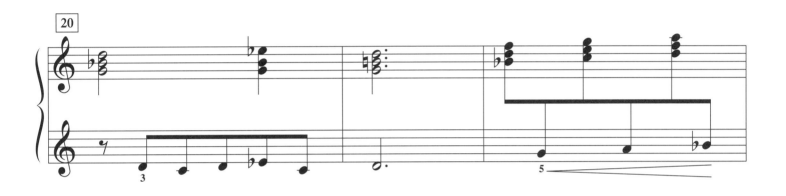

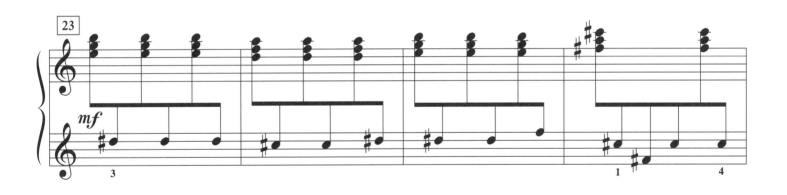

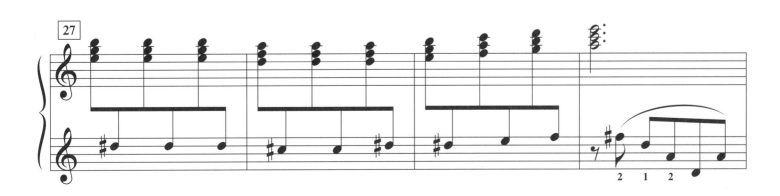

Secondo

Primo

Canon in D

Secondo

Johann Pachelbel
arr. Robert Schultz

FF1613

Canon in D

Primo

Johann Pachelbel
arr. Robert Schultz

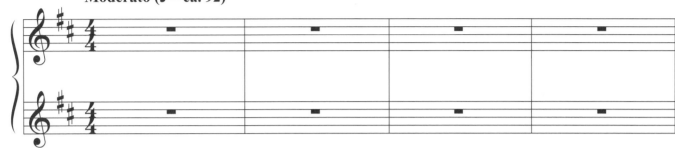

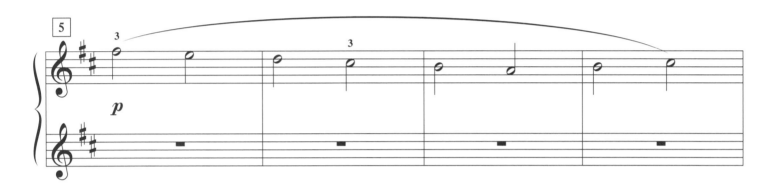

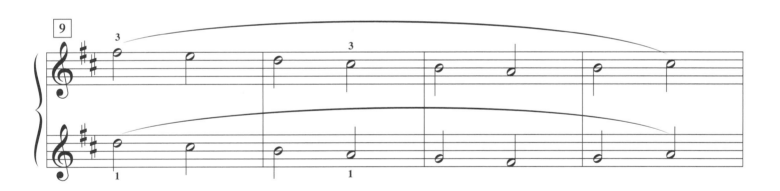

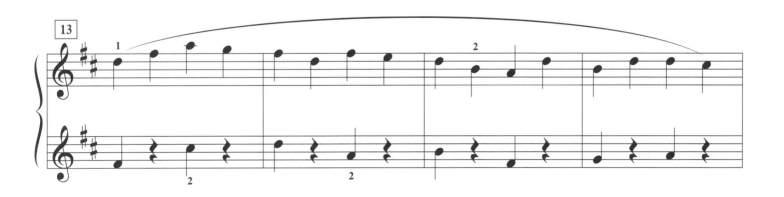

Secondo

Primo

Secondo

Primo

Secondo

Primo

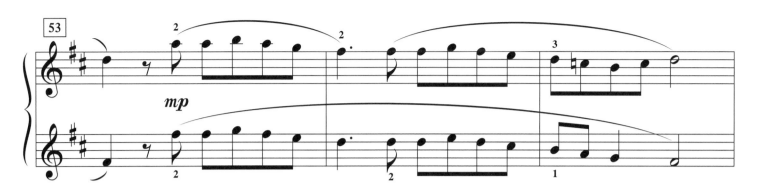

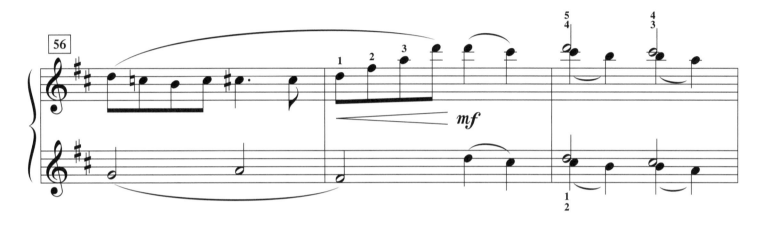

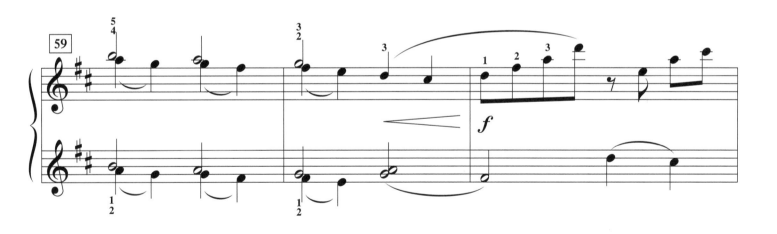

Melody Bober

Piano instructor, music teacher, composer, clinician—Melody Bober has been active in music education for over 25 years. As a composer, her goal is to create exciting and challenging pieces that are strong teaching tools to promote a lifelong love, understanding, and appreciation for music. Pedagogy, ear training, and musical expression are fundamentals of Melody's teaching, as well as fostering composition skills in her students. Melody graduated with highest honors from the University of Illinois with a degree in music education, and later received a master's degree in piano performance. She maintains a large private studio, performs in numerous regional events, and conducts workshops across the country. She and her husband Jeff reside in Minnesota.

Timothy Brown

Composition has always been a natural form of self-expression for Timothy Brown. His Montessori-influenced philosophy has greatly helped define his approach as a teacher and composer of educational music. His composition originates from a love of improvisation at the piano and his personal goal of writing music that will help release the student's imagination.

Mr. Brown holds two degrees in piano performance, including a master's degree from the University of North Texas. His many honors include a "Commissioned for Clavier" magazine article, and first prize award in the Fifth Aliénor International Harpsichord Competition for his solo composition *Suite Española*. As a clinician, Mr. Brown has presented numerous clinics and most recently represented FJH Music with his presentation at the 2000 World Piano Pedagogy Conference. Currently living in Dallas, Mr. Brown teaches piano and composition at the Harry Stone Montessori Magnet School. He frequently serves as an adjudicator for piano and composition contests, and performs with his wife as duo-pianists.

Edwin McLean

Edwin McLean is a freelance composer living in Chapel Hill, North Carolina. He is a graduate of the Yale School of Music, where he studied with Krzysztof Penderecki and Jacob Druckman. He also holds a master's degree in music theory and a bachelor's degree in piano performance from the University of Colorado.

Mr. McLean has been the recipient of several grants and awards: The MacDowell Colony, the John Work Award, the Woods Chandler Prize (Yale), Meet the Composer, Florida Arts Council, and many others. He has also won the Aliénor Composition Competition for his work *Sonata for Harpsichord*, published by The FJH Music Company Inc. and recorded by Elaine Funaro (*Into the Millennium*, Gasparo GSCD-331).

Since 1979, Edwin McLean has arranged the music of some of today's best known recording artists. Currently, he is senior editor as well as MIDI orchestrator for FJH Music.

Kevin Olson

Kevin Olson is an active pianist, composer, and faculty member at Elmhurst College near Chicago, Illinois, where he teaches classical and jazz piano, music theory, and electronic music. He holds a Doctor of Education degree from National-Louis University, and bachelor's and master's degrees in music composition and theory from Brigham Young University. Before teaching at Elmhurst College, he held a visiting professor position at Humboldt State University in California.

A native of Utah, Kevin began composing at the age of five. When he was 12, his composition *An American Trainride* received the Overall First Prize at the 1983 National PTA Convention in Albuquerque, New Mexico. Since then, he has been a composer-in-residence at the National Conference on Piano Pedagogy and has written music for the American Piano Quartet, Chicago a cappella, the Rich Matteson Jazz Festival, and several piano teachers associations around the country.

Kevin maintains a large piano studio, teaching students of a variety of ages and abilities. Many of the needs of his own piano students have inspired over 40 books and solos published by The FJH Music Company Inc., which he joined as a writer in 1994.

Wynn-Anne Rossi

Wynn-Anne Rossi is a multi talented composer, pianist, and educator. According to the *Illinois Times*, which awarded her the accolade Best Piano Teacher, she is "about as conventional as her hyphenated first name."

A resident of Minnesota, Wynn-Anne has received commissions from Minnesota Public Radio, America Composers Forum, Minnesota Music Teachers Association, and a number of private institutions. She is currently being presented as a living woman composer by the Bravo Music Education Program, which introduces her original works to thousands of elementary children each year. She also enjoys presenting lectures and workshops for music organizations on various topics, including the art of incorporating original composition into piano study.

Educated at the University of Colorado in theory and composition, Wynn-Anne has traveled and lived throughout the United States. In Boston, she furthered her training at Harvard University. Although her first love is for piano music, she has written a wide variety of repertoire, including a futuristic ballet, children's liturgical music, text and music for vocal ensembles, and chamber music. Ms. Rossi continues to teach and compose in her private studio, where Max the dog, Boomer the cat, and the rest of her family provide her with plenty of inspiration. Her first CD, *Take Me North*, is currently available at rossi-music.com.

Valerie Roth Roubos

Valerie Roth Roubos earned degrees in music theory, composition, and flute performance from the University of Wyoming.

Ms. Roubos maintains a studio in her home in Spokane, Washington, where she teaches flute, piano, and composition. She is active as a performer, adjudicator, lecturer, and accompanist. She has lectured on various topics and taught master classes at the Washington State Music Teachers Conference, Holy Names Music Camp, and the Spokane and Tri-Cities chapters of WSMTA. Ms. Roubos has played an active role in the Spokane Music Teachers Association and the Washington State Music Teachers Association.

In 2001, the South Dakota Music Teachers Association selected her as Composer of the Year and with MTNA commissioned her to write *An American Portrait: Scenes from the Great Plains* published by The FJH Music Company Inc.

Ms. Roubos was chosen to be the 2004 – 2005 Composer in Residence at Washington State University. The Washington State Music Teachers Association selected her as the 2006 Composer of the Year.

Ms. Roubos' teaching philosophy and compositions reflect her belief that all students, from elementary to advanced, are capable of musical playing that incorporates sensitivity and expression. Her compositions represent a variety of musical styles, including sacred, choral, and educational piano works.

Robert Schultz

Robert Schultz, composer, arranger, and editor, has achieved international fame during his career in the music publishing industry. The Schultz Piano Library, established in 1980, has included more than 500 publications of classical works, popular arrangements, and Schultz's original compositions in editions for pianists of every level from the beginner through the concert artist. In addition to his extensive library of published piano works, Schultz's output includes original orchestral works, chamber music, works for solo instruments, and vocal music.

Schultz has presented his published editions at workshops, clinics, and convention showcases throughout the United States and Canada. He is a long-standing member of ASCAP and has served as president of the Miami Music Teachers Association. Mr. Schultz's original piano compositions and transcriptions are featured on the compact disc recordings *Visions of Dunbar* and *Tina Faigen Plays Piano Transcriptions*, released on the ACA Digital label and available worldwide. His published original works for concert artists are noted in Maurice Hinson's *Guide to the Pianist's Repertoire, Third Edition*. He currently devotes his full time to composing and arranging, writing from his studio in Miami, Florida. In-depth information about Robert Schultz and The Schultz Piano Library is available at the Web site www.schultzmusic.com.

A great way to prepare for your duet performances is to use the CD in the following ways:

1) Listen to the complete performances of all of the pieces. In this way, you will understand the different styles and personalities of each of the pieces. Enjoy listening to these duets anywhere, anytime! Listen to them casually (as background music) or attentively. After you have listened to the CD, you might discuss interpretation with your teacher and follow along with your score as you listen.

About the *primo* and *secondo* parts: (These Italian music terms are pronounced "PREE-moh" and "seh-KOHN-doh")

Remember that the *primo* part is always on the right-hand side of the book, while the *secondo* part is always on the left-hand side of the book. The *primo* part usually stays above middle C, while the *secondo* part usually stays below middle C.

2) The CD can be used as a practice partner, because you can play along with the performances.

Playing along with the performance track encourages flexibility in rhythm and musicality, because the pianists are playing as if in a performance and not with the metronome. This is exactly what will occur when you are performing with a duet partner. Be sure that you practice your duet part by itself, with the metronome, before you attempt to play along with the performance track and before you rehearse with your partner.